MODELS

Keith Newell

SEA-TO-SEA

Mankato Collingwood London

This edition first published in 2006 by
Sea-to-Sea Publications
1980 Lookout Drive
North Mankato
Minnesota 56003

Copyright © Sea-to-Sea Publications 2006

Printed in China

Library of Congress Cataloging-in-Publication Data

Newell, Keith.
  Models/ by Keith Newell.
    p. cm − (Art and craft skills)
  ISBN 1-932889-85-X
  1. Modeling−Juvenile literature. 2. Paper sculpture−Juvenile literature. 3.
Papier-mâché−Juvenile literature. I. Title. II. Art and craft skills (North Mankato, Minn.)

TT916.N48 2005
745.5−dc22

                                                2004063711

9 8 7 6 5 4 3 2

Published by arrangement with the Watts Publishing Group Ltd., London

Project designer and model maker: Keith Newell
Series editor: Kyla Barber
Designer: Richard Langford
Art director: Robert Walster
Illustrator: Peter Bull
Photographer: Steve Shott
Cake maker: Barbara Osborn

Contents

Getting Started

Model making, or "sculpture," is a form of art, but instead of using a flat surface—as you do when you paint—you are working in "3-D" or "three dimensions."

Before you start you need to decide three things:
1. **SUBJECT**—what you are going to make
2. **STRUCTURE**—how you are going to build it
3. **MATERIALS**—what you are going to use to build it

Basic Methods

1. Molding: This is when you make an object by shaping a soft material, such as clay. It can be rolled into strips and coiled around or molded directly into a shape.

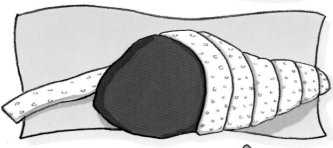

2. Framework: Sometimes you need to build your model around a frame. You must make sure the frame is strong enough to support your sculpture.

3. Construction: This is where you build your model by joining all your materials together—without building a frame first.

4

MODELING TIPS

❖ Before you begin, prepare all your materials and clear a working area.

❖ Subjects are all around you—use your imagination.

❖ Simple models can be just as effective as more complicated ones.

❖ Alter the scale: If the subject you are copying is small—make your model huge, if it is big—make yours tiny.

❖ You can work with more than one material—try mixing them.

❖ You can build your object any way you like. There are no rules.

Building a Frame

1. Assemble your materials. Make sure you have everything you need.

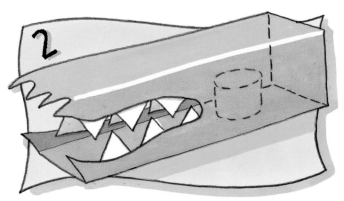

2. Join them together to make up the basic shape.

3. Cover the frame with your chosen materials—clay, papier–mâché, fabric, or whatever you want!

Modeling Supplies

The basic items listed below include everything you need to do the projects in this book. The store key shows you where to get them.

Store key

Art supply store

Craft or hobby store

Drug store

Supermarket

Stationery store

Toy store

Making Models

1. Newspaper—use for papier–mâché and for stuffing.

2. Old cardboard boxes for creating structures. Free from ( ).

3. A variety of food–packaging materials—egg cartons, drinks' cartons, plastic pots. Free from ( ).

4. Cardboard—thick and thin, in a variety of colors and textures ( ).

5. Clay is cheap and very easy to find. Use it for molding ( ).

6. Plaster cloth is simple to use, and is quick and effective ( ).

7. Flour and salt can be combined to make salt dough—a very cheap and useful material for molding ( ).

8. Add eggs, milk, and sugar to flour and you can make a cake mixture—great for edible models! ( ).

9. Sand, shells, and pebbles can be used to make water scenes.

10. Plasticine is useful for making a mold over which you can use papier–mâché, or layer on plaster cloth ( ).

11. Glass bottles such as oil or food–coloring bottles ( ).

Covering and Wrapping

12. Fabric—use up bits and pieces from old clothes, tag sales, or remnants in fabric shops.

13. Bubble wrap can be painted and used to cover your models (⬡ ⬡).

14. Kitchen foil and cling wrap for covering and wrapping (🛒).

Painting and Decorating

15. Paints—poster paints, watercolors, block paints, fabric paints, or acrylic paints. Check the maker's instructions when deciding which to use (⬡ ⬡ ⬡ ⬡).

16. A range of brushes for different-sized projects (⬡ ⬡ ⬡ ⬡).

17. Gold and silver spray paint and glitter for jazzing up small items (⬡ ⬡).

18. Varnish—you can buy some or, better still, mix up some water-thinned white glue (⬡ ⬡ ⬡).

19. Food dye can be used to color cake mixture, cream, icing, or water (🛒).

20. Stores often give away brightly colored plastic bags. Cut them into strips and use for decoration.

Art Box Basics

21. White glue for sticking large areas and for varnishing (see above) (⬡ ⬡ ⬡ ⬡).

22. Glue stick for sticking small areas (⬡ ⬡ ⬡).

23. String and sewing kit (⬡).

24. Metal wire—for frameworks (⬡).

25. Masking tape and sticky tape (⬡ ⬡).

26. Scissors and craft knife—use with an adult's help (⬡ ⬡).

27. Metal ruler for measuring, cutting, and scoring (⬡ ⬡).

Construction

Gather together boxes, packaging, plastic bottles—anything you can find . Assemble, then paint them in bright colors. This "construction" method of modeling is simple but effective. Try this totem pole.

You Will Need

- ❏ five cardboard boxes
- ❏ white glue
- ❏ egg carton
- ❏ oaktag
- ❏ paints and brushes
- ❏ plastic bottle or carton
- ❏ thread
- ❏ colored plastic bag
- ❏ yogurt container
- ❏ thick cardboard
- ❏ two sticky tape inner tubes (or similar)
- ❏ kitchen foil
- ❏ scissors

Glue five boxes together, in a tower. Glue on a plastic bottle for a nose, an egg carton for a mouth, sunglasses for the eyes. Roll tubes from oaktag for arms and add strips from a plastic bag to the ends. Now paint.

Fish Mobile

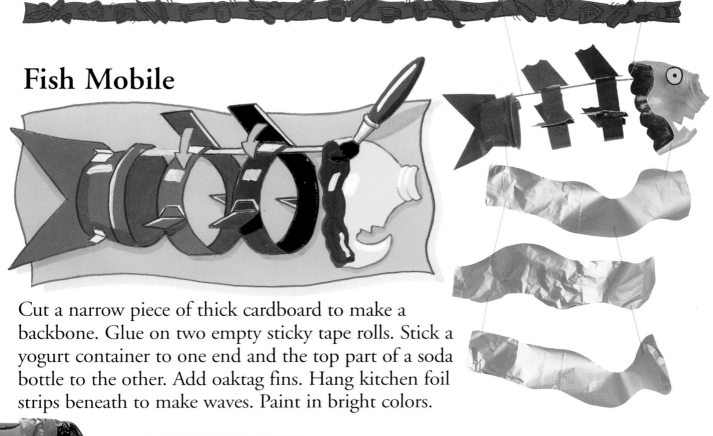

Cut a narrow piece of thick cardboard to make a backbone. Glue on two empty sticky tape rolls. Stick a yogurt container to one end and the top part of a soda bottle to the other. Add oaktag fins. Hang kitchen foil strips beneath to make waves. Paint in bright colors.

Now Try This

Dragon Puppet

Cut out a dragon's head from a long box (see instruction for building a frame on page 5). Cut a mouth shape and add oaktag teeth. Make a neck from a poster tube or some rolled-up oaktag. Stick the head on the neck. Cover it in green–painted bubble wrap for a scaly effect. Cover the base of the neck in a trash bag. Roll up a red plastic bag to make a fiery tongue.

Using Water

You can include many different materials in your models—including water. But to use a liquid, you first must find a suitable container. To make this beach scene we added colored water to sand in a plastic tub.

1. Find a large transparent container such as an ice cream tub. Fill half with sand and shape it into a beach. Add packing material or strips cut from a plastic bag for seaweed.

2. Make a lighthouse. Roll up a tube of oaktag about 6 in (15cm) long. Stick the base into a plasticine mound. Paint and then varnish with water–thinned white glue. Stick a cork in the top.

You Will Need

- clear plastic container
- water and pitcher
- paints and brush
- colored plastic bag
- cork (optional)
- plasticine   ◆ sand
- blue food dye ◆ oaktag
- plastic animals ◆ scissors
- white glue

3. Fill a pitcher with about a quart (liter) of water. Add blue food dye. Pour into the container. Add plastic animals.

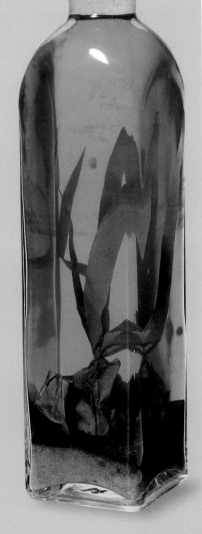

Bottle Garden
Find a glass or plastic bottle. Soak in warm soapy water for 15 minutes and peel off the label. Add a layer of sand. Cut strips from a plastic bag and weigh them down with plasticine. Drop them into the bottle. Fill with blue-dyed water.

Mini Bottle Shaker
Find a small bottle with a cap. Fill it with water. Add colored glitter. Tighten the lid. Shake!

Framework

To make this life-sized model of a "wild man" create a strong frame from cardboard, then add clothes, twigs, and leaves.

You Will Need

- ☆ large sheets of strong cardboard
- ☆ toilet roll tubes
- ☆ paint
- ☆ cardboard boxes
- ☆ newspaper
- ☆ old shirt
- ☆ paint brushes
- ☆ old pair of pants
- ☆ scissors
- ☆ old pair of shoes (optional)

1. Roll up strong cardboard into tubes for the legs. Make them long enough to fit in some old pants. Pad around the tubes with scrunched-up newspaper.

2. Stand the base of each tube in an old shoe. You might need to lean your wild man against a wall to keep him standing up.

3. Put a cardboard box in the shirt and pad it out with newspaper, then place it on top of the legs.

4. Make a mask by cutting out a face from cardboard. Use toilet roll tubes cut in half lengthwise for the features. Paint and add twigs and leaves for the hair.

Now Try This

Robin Hood Hat
Create a frame for the hat by rolling up some newspaper to make a cone, and securing it with sticky tape. Take an old T-shirt and wrap the cone in the material. Use an old sock to make a brim for the hat. Add a feather or a badge to the front.

Edible Sculptures

Many foods can be shaped, colored and decorated—so why not make an edible model? Bake a sponge cake and turn it into this mermaid.

You Will Need

- ❖ cake ❖ knife ❖ mixing bowls
- ❖ cream ❖ cake pan ❖ food dyes
- ❖ water ❖ wire whisk ❖ spoon
- ❖ butter cream—beat butter and sugar together ❖ icing sugar ❖ wax paper
- ❖ piping bag ❖ sugar balls, glacé cherries

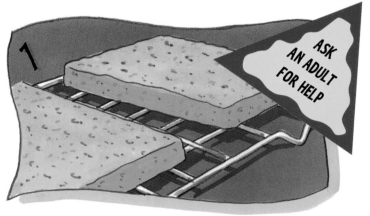

ASK AN ADULT FOR HELP

1. Follow a recipe for a simple sponge cake and bake two layers of cake. Cool, then sandwich them with butter cream.

2. Draw the outline of a mermaid on some wax paper. Cut it out and lay it on top of the cake. Cut around the outline. Cover the cake's top and sides with butter cream.

Icing Painting and Fish Cakes

With the spare bits of cake you can make other edible sculptures.

3. Keep a little white icing sugar for the eyes. Color half of the rest pink and half green. Drop a tiny amount of food dye and knead the color into the icing sugar. Roll out and lay over the cake. Add the eyes.

Cut out a house shape and dribble colored icing from a spoon onto a paper plate to complete the picture.

4. Make up some more butter cream. Color some of it yellow for the hair and the rest blue for the sea. Use a piping bag if you have one. Draw a smile with food dye.

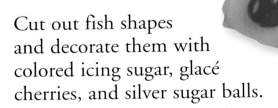

Cut out fish shapes and decorate them with colored icing sugar, glacé cherries, and silver sugar balls.

Salt Dough

Salt dough is simply made from flour, salt, and water. It is easy to mold, and once it has dried it can be painted and varnished for spectacular results. Make a devilish, winged gargoyle to hang on your wall.

You Will Need

★ flour   ★ salt   ★ water
★ glass   ★ board   ★ paints
★ rolling pin   ★ brushes
★ white glue   ★ measuring cup
★ stiff brown cardboard
★ mixing sppon ★ bowl

To harden your salt dough, ask an adult to cook it in the oven for 8 hours at the lowest setting. Or you can let it dry for 24 hours.

1. Mix 4 cups of flour with two cups of salt. Add water slowly until the dough is stiff, but not sticky.

2. Knead the dough for about ten minutes, then place on a flat board.

16

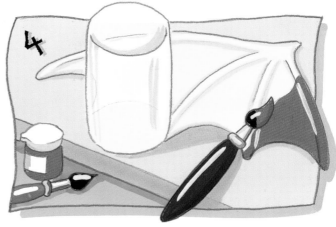

3. Mold your gargoyle's face. Use extra bits of dough to make teeth, horns, and a tongue. Make it as ugly and frightening as you can!

4. Roll out more dough and mold it into the shape of wings, using a glass to cut out the curves. Bake in the oven or let them dry. Paint and varnish with water-thinned white glue.

To make the gargoyle look like it is bursting through the wall, glue on small jagged pieces of brown cardboard to create a splintered wood effect.

Now Try These

Gargoyle Mirror
Find an old mirror, then make up some salt dough. Make each gargoyle separately and stick it on to the mirror's edge next to the previous one. Finish with a pair of wings. Smooth over the joins with your fingers and bake or let it dry.

Salt Dough Banana
Make up some salt dough and mold it into the shape of a banana with the skin peeled back. Bake or let dry, then paint the banana and skin.

Reuse and Redecorate

A collection of old toys makes a great starting point for model making. Add glitter and shiny paints to brighten them up, then try combining them with other modeling materials.

You Will Need

- ❖ small old toys
- ❖ brushes
- ❖ glitter
- ❖ gold or silver paint or spray
- ❖ white glue
- ❖ salt   ❖ flour   ❖ water
- ❖ bowl
- ❖ hair barrettes, earring fixtures, or safety pins   ❖ mixing spoon

Stick toys onto a barrette.

Add a safety pin to m a badge.

Paint on metallic colors and make earrings.

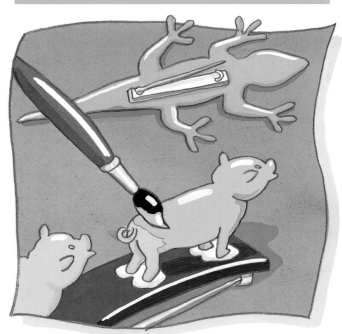

Pick out some old toys, such as cars or farmyard animals, and glue them on to hair barrettes or make them into earrings or badges. Spray or paint them with gold and silver, or cover them in glitter.

Picture Frame

Combine your salt dough molding techniques (see page 16) with your redecorated toys and make truly original picture frames.

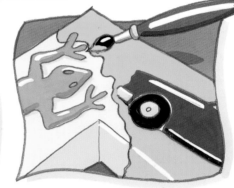

1. Make up the salt dough and mold four sides of a frame. Join them together.

2. Pick out several small toys and push them into the dough.

3. Let the frame dry for a day, then paint it with gold paint.

Plaster Cloth

Plaster cloth comes in sheets and is like the material doctors use to make casts for broken bones. The sheets are dipped in water and laid over a mold. They stick together and harden in only a few minutes to form a strong, rigid shape. Try this American Indian bird.

You Will Need

- plasticine
- water
- brushes
- craft knife
- scissors
- trash bag
- plaster cloth
- paints
- white glue
- bowl

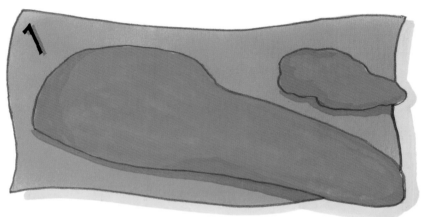

1. Find a kitchen bowl the size of your head. Mold plasticine over the top half of it to form a head shape. Take it off the bowl and add a long beak.

2. Cut strips of plaster cloth and soak in water for 30 seconds. Layer the strips of plaster cloth onto the mold.

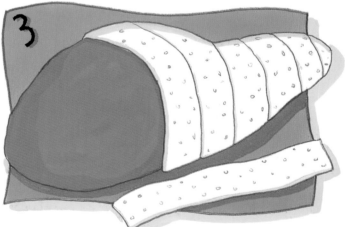

3. Keep adding strips until the whole head shape is covered. Let dry. Very gently lift the mask off the mold.

4. Ask an adult to cut holes for the nostrils with a craft knife. Paint, then varnish with water-thinned white glue.

5. Cut a black trash bag into strips and tie together at one end. Glue this to the top of the bird's head.

Now Try These

Mud Mask
Use plaster cloth to build up a mask over a plasticine mold. Paint and decorate with ethnic patterns and colors.

Underwater Scene
Soak strips of plaster cloth in water, then lay them on a flat surface. Scrunch them up slightly and drop on powder paint. Let dry. Paint on small fish.

ASK AN ADULT FOR HELP

Fabric Fun

Instead of painting or varnishing you can use material to bring all sorts of different textures, colors, and patterns to a 3–D object. Wrap, cover, or pad a shape with fabric. Use fur, felt, and cardboard to make this unusual clock.

You Will Need

- cardboard
- plate
- pencil
- scissors
- newspaper
- fabric
- felt—green and pink
- white glue
- clock movement and battery set or cut out clock hands from black cardboard
- plant pot and soil
- drawing pin

If you don't have a clock movement set you can cut out the hands of the clock from stiff black cardboard.

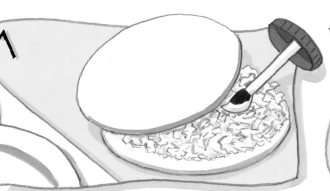

1. Cut out two circles in thick cardboard (draw around a plate). Scrunch up newspaper, stick it on to one of the circles and glue the second circle on top.

2. Cut a circle from fabric 2 in (5cm) larger than the cardboard circles. Cut eight slits, about 1 in (3cm) long, in from the edge. Glue the flaps of material to the top of the cardboard sandwich.

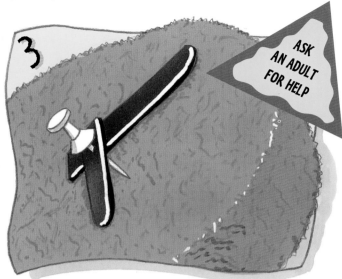

ASK AN ADULT FOR HELP

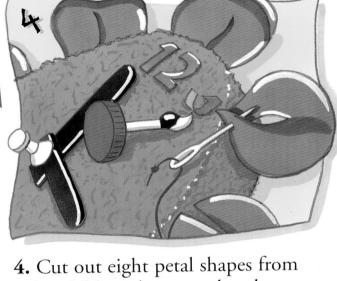

3. Cut a square hole in the back of the clock and slot the battery housing in. Turn the clock around, and from the front, push in the set of hands and slot them into the battery housing.

4. Cut out eight petal shapes from colored felt and sew or glue them to the outside edge of the clock face. Cut out numbers 1 to 12 in cardboard and glue them on the face.

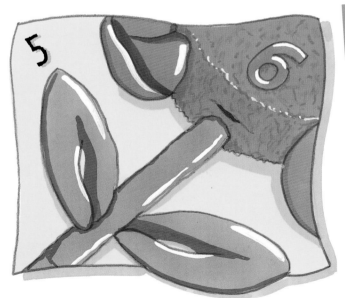

5. Tightly roll up a piece of cardboard. Wrap it in green felt to make a stem. Add leaves. Cut a slit in the bottom of the clock face. Push the stem in. Stand the stem in a plant pot packed with soil.

Now Try This

Fabric and Clay Puppets

Use fabric to give these clay puppets a furry body. Start by modeling a head out of clay or salt dough. Push a finger-sized hole into the base. Add wire or cocktail sticks for whiskers. Let dry, then paint the features. Cut out a square of fabric, then cut a hole in the middle large enough for your finger.

Paper Folding

This beetle is made using a simple technique, but it needs careful measuring and cutting.

You Will Need

- ❖ pencil
- ❖ ruler
- ❖ glue
- ❖ oaktag
- ❖ scissors
- ❖ sheets of thick colored paper
- ❖ double-sided sticky tape

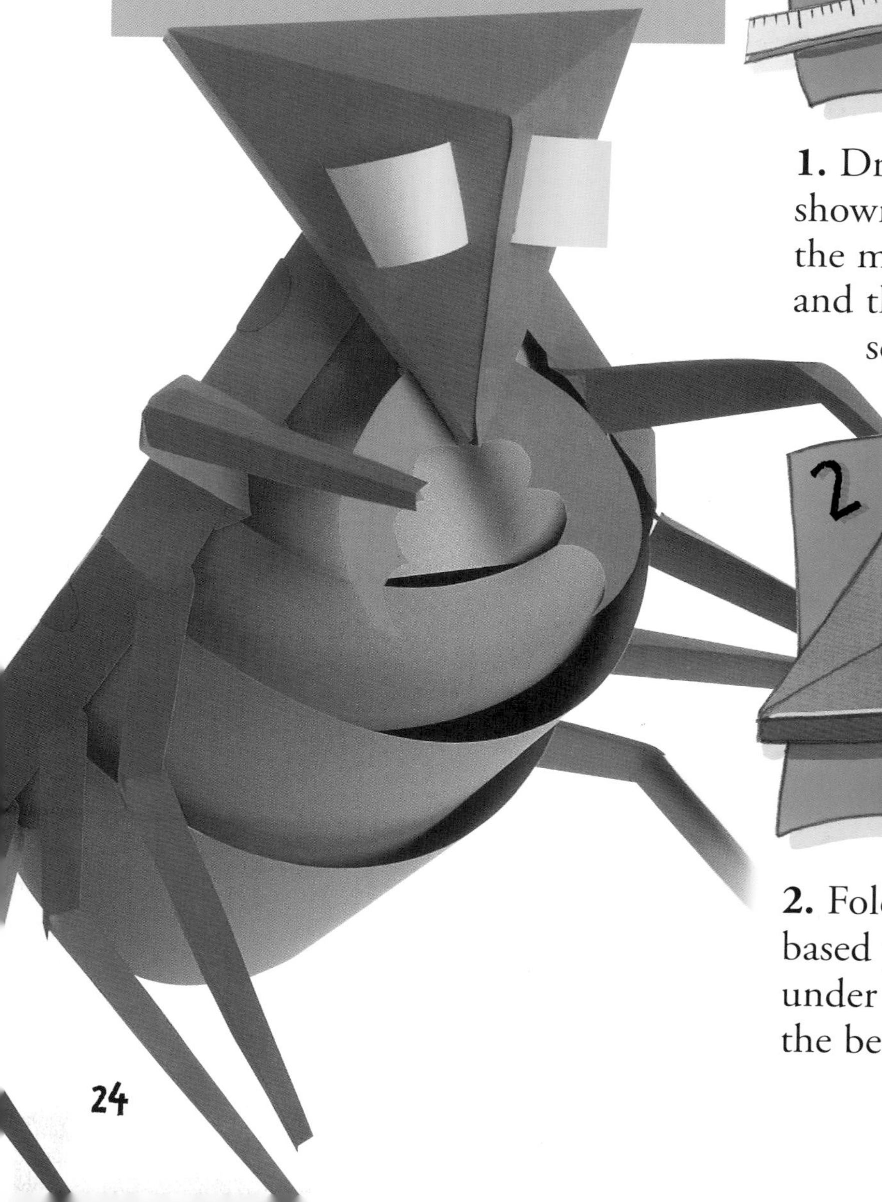

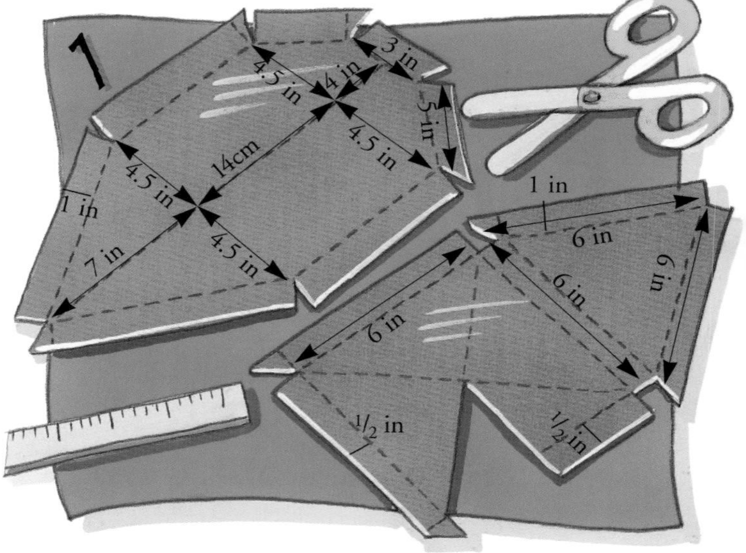

1. Draw the shapes in pencil as shown. Measure carefully. Cut along the main lines. Then, using a ruler and the back of a pair of scissors, score along the dotted lines. Fold the shapes as shown.

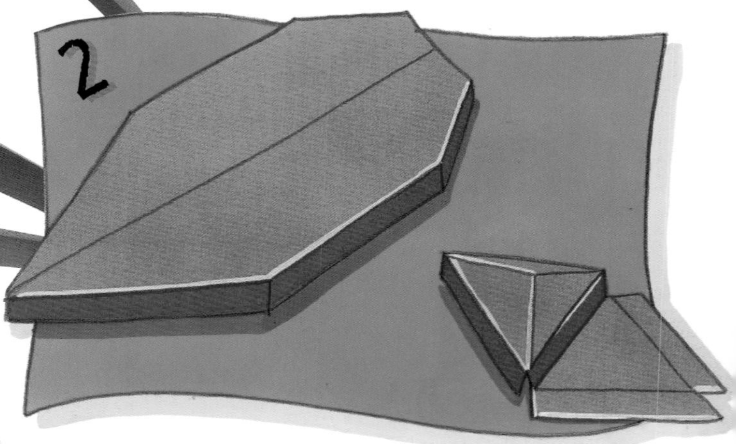

2. Fold the head into a triangular-based pyramid and glue the base under as shown. Then fold and stick the beetle's body edges into position.

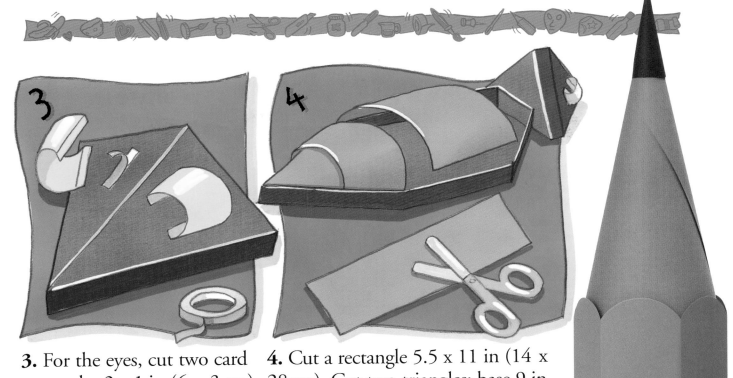

3. For the eyes, cut two card rectangles 2 x 1 in (6 x 3 cm). Curve and glue them to the sides of the head. Glue the head on the body.

4. Cut a rectangle 5.5 x 11 in (14 x 28 cm). Cut two triangles: base 9 in (24cm), sides 8 in (20cm). Cut off top third of each, throw away one top. Curve and glue them as shown.

5. Cut eight thin oaktag triangles 8 in (20 cm) long. Score along dotted lines. Fold in half lengthwise, then widthwise. Glue the legs to the body.

Now Try This

Giant Pencil

Take a large piece of coloured oaktag. Divide it widthwise into eight by drawing seven equally spaced vertical lines. Score and fold along each line and glue the edges together. For the point make a cone in yellow paper and glue it on the top of the tube. Make a smaller cone from black paper and glue it on top of the yellow one.

Clay Models

Clay can be used to build up a shape, or it can be wrapped around an existing frame. Combine both these methods to make this rocket lamp.

You Will Need

✧ blunt knife ✧ clay ✧ scissors ✧ ruler
✧ pastry cutter ✧ paint and brushes
✧ old lamp shade ✧ rolling pin and board
✧ pencil ✧ paper ✧ compasses ✧ white glue

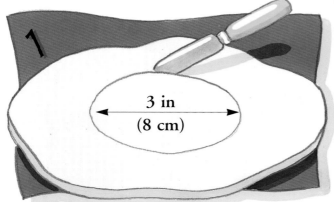

3 in
(8 cm)

1. Roll out a sheet of clay 0.4 in (1cm) thick. Draw a 3 in (8 cm) circle on paper. Cut it out. Place the circle over the clay. Using a blunt knife, cut out the circle of clay.

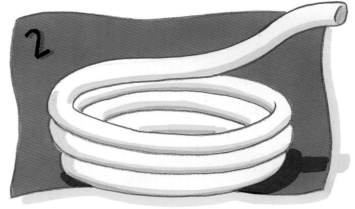

2. Roll out a thin sausage of clay—7 in (17 cm) long. Coil the sausage around the outside of the clay circle. Add a second coil on top of the first.

3. Add longer and longer coils to make the lamp base wider. After about eight coils start making them shorter each time, to make the base narrower.

4. Smooth over the clay. Add rocket details and push out a hole for the wire at the bottom. Let dry. Decorate using paint mixed with white glue.

5. Measure the shade frame at a, b, and c, and cut three pieces of clay to fit. Use a pastry cutter to press out moon and star shapes. Put the clay sheets on the frame and smooth over the edges. Let dry. Decorate with paint mixed with white glue.

ADULT HELP
Ask an adult to attach the lamp fitting, plug and wire.

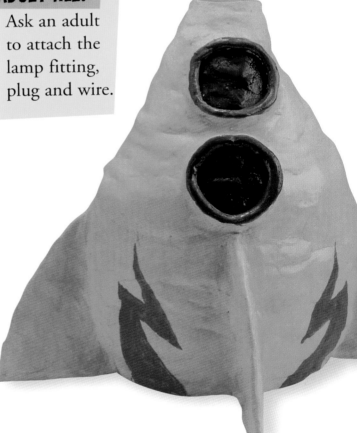

Now Try This

Necklace
Roll out some clay. Draw a heart on oaktag. Cut it out and use it as a template to cut around. Make a hole in the top of each heart with a pencil. Let dry, then paint and varnish. Thread string through the hearts.

Papier–Mâché

This whole puppy puppet is made from newspaper—from the mold to the papier–mâché covering.

You Will Need

- newspaper
- two small balls
- scissors
- sticky tape
- paints
- glue
- cling wrap
- flour and water
- craft knife
- spoon
- brush
- string
- coat hanger
- bowl
- pin

1. Scrunch up three balls of newspaper: one for the body, one for the head, and one for the snout. Wrap with tape. Stick the snout to the head.

2. Mix flour and water to make a creamy paste. Dip strips of newspaper into the mixture and layer them onto the body and head.

ASK AN ADULT FOR HELP

3. Make two shapes for the ears and four ovals for the feet in the same way. For the eyes, cover two small balls with papier–mâché. When dry, cut papier–mâché in half, pull the ball out, and glue halves back together.

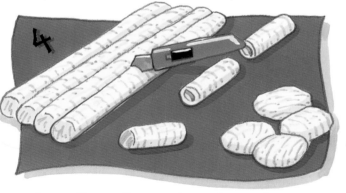

4. Roll up five tight tubes of newspaper. Cover each with cling wrap then papier–mâché over the top. When dry, slide the papier–mâché off. Cut four tubes in half for the legs, and one tube into three for the tail.

★ Paint each section and let dry. Attach string to link all the sections of the legs and the tail together and to attach them to the body. To tie string to the papier–mâché, use a pin to make two holes close together, then thread string in one hole and out the other. Tie the ends. Attach strings from the head and the back of the body. Tie them to a coat hanger.

Now Try These

Alien Mask
Make a mold of an alien's face in plasticine. Cover the mold with one layer of tissue paper dipped in water. This will allow you to peel the mask off the mold. Add four layers of tissue dipped in a flour and water paste. When dry, peel off gently, then paint and varnish.

Bowl
Cover a balloon with papier–mâché to about halfway (you can leave a straight or a jagged edge). Let dry, then burst the balloon. Paint and varnish, or cover over the papier–mâché with a collage of pictures cut from magazines.

29

Mixing Media

Try mixing all kinds of different materials together. This bone throne uses cardboard, fabric, paper, clay, and papier-mâché.

You Will Need

- ❏ large box
- ❏ newspaper
- ❏ flour and water
- ❏ sticky tape
- ❏ strong cardboard
- ❏ old magazines
- ❏ craft knife
- ❏ glue
- ❏ oaktag
- ❏ wire coat hanger
- ❏ clay
- ❏ paint
- ❏ brushes
- ❏ pencil
- ❏ wire cutter

1. Find a large, strong box and weight it down with old magazines. Cut a strong piece of cardboard to form a backbone.

2. Cut a slit in the box and slide in the cardboard. Add ribs made from rolled up newspaper.

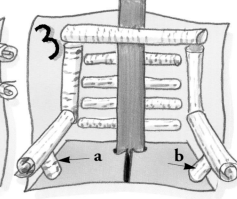

a
b

3. Roll up oaktag tubes—two for the legs, one for the shoulders, and four for the arms. Glue in place and support with tubes a and b.

4. Make a skull using the papier-mâché bowl technique on page 29. Draw on details or hollow them out. Tape the skull to the backbone and paint it all.

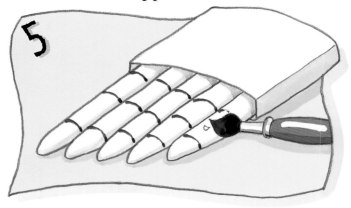

5. Make feet out of oaktag and paint them. Glue them on to the legs. You can make the hands in the same way, or you can use the method opposite.

Hands

ASK AN ADULT FOR HELP

Ask an adult to cut ten pieces from a wire coat hanger. Make three clay finger joints for each finger, and two for the thumb. Push the joints on to the wire. Dry, then paint them.

MODELING TIP

Sew fabric on to the box for the hip bones and on to the shoulders for shoulder blades.

What Next?

Try remaking some of the projects in this book, using different materials—or using a mixture of materials. Try:

● the puppy puppet on page 29 from folded paper

● the American Indian bird on page 21 from salt dough and fabric

● the gargoyle on page 16 from cake mixture and icing

● the mermaid on page 14 from papier-mâché.

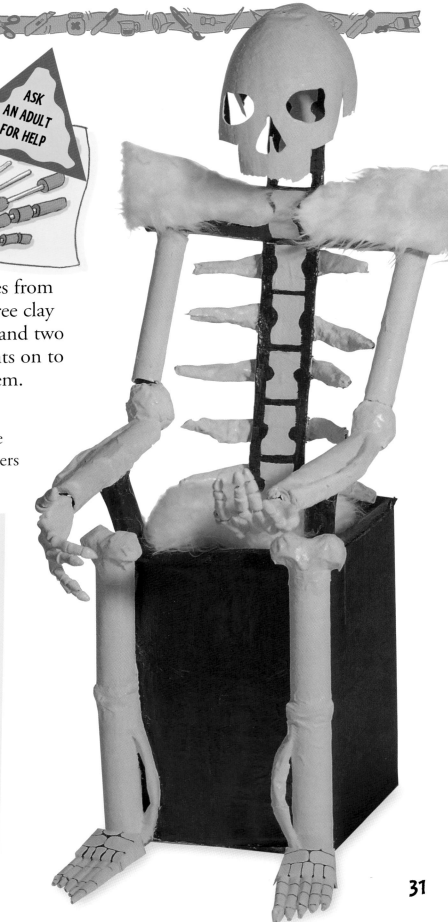

Glossary

framework The skeleton of a model (pages 4, 5).

knead To press and work dough using your hands (page 16).

medium The material used to make a model, you can use one medium, or several (page 30).

mold Shape a model using a soft material such as clay or plasticine (pages 4, 20, 26).

papier–mâché A technique of building up a shape using strips of paper soaked in glue and water (pages 5, 28, 30).

reuse To use something again after it has already been used for its original purpose (page 18).

score To mark a line on a piece of cardboard with a pair of scissors to make it easier to fold (page 24).

sculpture A 3–D (three-dimensional) piece of art (page 4).

subject The item that you are copying when you make your model or paint your picture (pages 4, 5).

template An outline that can be used to draw around so that the pattern or shape can be repeated exactly several times (page 27).

texture The look or feel of a surface (page 22).

three-dimensional (3–D) Used to describe an object that is not just flat, but has depth as well (pages 4, 22).

Index

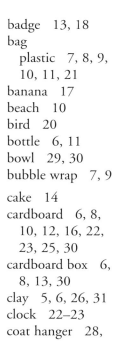